The Meeting

The Meeting: www.brookes.ac.uk/the-meeting

First published in 2020
by the John Clare Society
c/o Simon Kövesi, Oxford Brookes University, Oxford, OX3 0BP

Design and tyepsetting by Lee Meads at Rather Fine Design,
www.ratherfinedesign.co.uk

Cover art by Mitch Miller, www.dialectograms.com

Printed by Joshua Horgan, 2, Glenmore Business Centre,
Range Road, Witney OX29 0AA
www.joshuahorgan.co.uk

John Clare Society: www.johnclaresociety.wordpress.com

ISBN 978-1-9161355-2-9

The Meeting
Reading and Writing through John Clare

Edited by SIMON KÖVESI

Poetry editors

SARAH CORBETT
JOHN GALLAS
KAREN MCCARTHY WOOLF
CLARE SHAW

John Clare Society
2020

CONTENTS

THE MEETING.

HERE we meet, too soon to part,
Here to leave will raise a smart,
Here I'll press thee to my heart,
    Where none have place above thee :
Here I vow to love thee well,
And could words unseal the spell,
Had but language strength to tell,
    I'd say how much I love thee.

Here, the rose that decks thy door,
Here, the thorn that spreads thy bow'r,
Here, the willow on the moor,
    The birds at rest above thee,
Had they light of life to see,
Sense of soul like thee and me
Soon might each a witness be
    How doatingly I love thee,

By the night-sky's purple ether,
And by even's sweetest weather,
That oft has blest us both together,—
    The moon that shines above thee,
And shews thy beauteous cheek so blooming,
And by pale age's winter coming,
The charms, and casualties of woman,
    I will for ever love thee.

Facsimile of 'The Meeting', from *Poems Descriptive of Rural Life and Scenery*
(London: Taylor and Hessey, 1820), pp. xxiii–iv.

Introduction

Simon Kövesi

This book is the culmination of a project which started with a simple question: why and how does John Clare appeal to so many creative artists? From 1820 – the year his first book was published – Clare was almost immediately the recipient of dedicatory poems. *Poems Descriptive of Rural Life and Scenery* was published in London in January; the very first poem in it – 'The Meeting' – was set to an original composition and sung on the West End stage in an opera, as quickly as February. And two hundred years later, the variety of forms in which people creatively respond to Clare – seek dialogue with his words – seek to bring his concerns, his topics, his styles, his voices, his sounds and songs – into contemporary currency – is all of it quite astonishing when considered in the round. Musicians, visual artists, novelists, playwrights, filmmakers, actors, storytellers and poets: all seem to be persistently curious about Clare. Increasingly, natural historians, journalists and the ever-widening commentariat are turning to him too.

But why? The seemingly passionate sincerity of his Romantic confessional mode, the accuracy and specificity of his natural history, the uniqueness and locality of his voice, his class and the commonality and universality of his concerns, the musicality of his rhyming line, even his apparent depression (or 'blue devils' as he labelled it) and decades-long institionalisation in asylums[1] – so many facets of his life and work seem to ripple with fresh relevancy across artistic, creative practice. And sadly enough our environmentally-challenged times can, in Clare, find someone who functions almost as an early warning siren, especially through his protest polemics, those celebrated poems railing against enclosure (the efficiency-driven governmental reorganisation of rural land) and more generally through his constant vocal attention to the neglect, abuse and degradation of nature, which seems always to be the result of civilisation's 'onward' march. Of course, 'improvement' did not end with enclosure, even for Clare. He looked back to the long history of exploitation, in a poem such as 'The Lament of Swordy Well' – the speaking voice of which is a piece of land, quarried and used for all kinds of purposes, as far back as the Romans. Swordy Well is exposed to the ravages of exploitation, especially when food prices rise:

> The silver springs grown naked dykes
> Scarce own a bunch of rushes
> When grain got high the tasteless tykes
> Grubbed up trees banks and bushes
> And me they turned me inside out
> For sand and grit and stones
> And turned my old green hills about
> And pickt my very bones

Clare worries about all natural life, each element of it integrated with, and dependent upon, the next. When the land is harmed, the wildlife suffers:

> The bees flye round in feeble rings
> And find no blossom bye
> Then thrum their almost weary wings
> Upon the moss and die
> Rabbits that find my hills turned oer
> Forsake my poor abode
> They dread a workhouse like the poor
> And nibble on the road[2]

Clare's knowledge of the complexities of the natural world remains unparalleled in English poetry. His awareness of its fragility in the face of humanity's inventiveness, offers lessons useful even now. On Saturday 4 June 1825, he noted in his journal:

> Saw three fellows at the end of Royce wood who I found were laying out the plan for an 'Iron rail way' from Manchester to London – it is to cross over Round Oak Spring by Royce Wood Corner for Woodcroft Castle I little thought that fresh intrusions woud interupt and spoil my solitudes after the Inclosure they will despoil a boggy place that is famous for Orchises at Royce Wood end[3]

The big national plan threatens all the local characters – places Clare knew as old, intimate friends, all around his village of Helpston, in Northamptonshire (the village is now in Cambridgeshire, county boundaries having shifted). Clare is worried here, but in truth he could have no idea what was to come. It is important to remember that his gradually industrialising times were very different to our own. When human life was tough and disappointing, Clare could turn to certainty in nature, security in his relationship with an ineluctable return, a confident hope, offered by the promise of spring, even in the depths of a long winter.

Clare had no sense that nature was finite, nor could he have had the same basic conception we do, of the entire world being vulnerable to man. Nevertheless there is still sharp prescience in constant alertness to the ways we 'despoil' local treasures in the pursuit of large-scale industry, and in his acute sensitivity to, and botanical awareness of, the fragility of what we now call ecosystems. And al of his alertness to a fragile world is expressed through a unique voice – a labouring-class language full of local dialect terms – in which, for example, a snail is a 'pooty', a herring gull is a 'cawdymawdy', a mole is a 'mouldiwarp', and where someone 'drowking' is someone drooping from drought, after a hard day in the fields. Clare's world is one of work: of muddy fields, stormy skies, miserable poverty. Yet glimmers of hope and respite, he finds here and there, among the back-breaking burdens of 'common' people – ordinary working folk, too often ignored by the literary arts. Clare's written world is accessible, playfully aware of literary history, of its forms and styles, combining that wide reading with a unique understanding of ballad and folk culture; common custom and local myth. He offers a rare mix, for sure. And for these and many other reasons, people of all stripes discover and return to Clare again and again, refashioning and remaking him as they go.

This project was set up in two parts: firstly, across early 2019, it sought to get established poets with deep knowledge of, and sympathy for, Clare, to inspire new poetry, in new poets, in new situations, through close critical attention to his world and work. Consulting initially with the National Literacy Trust to determine areas of literary (and literacy) need, and drawing on generous financial support from Oxford Brookes University, we targeted four locations and four brilliant local libraries in which to set up shop. Sarah Corbett ran free workshops in Bradford and Keighley libraries; John Gallas did the same in Peterborough Central Library; Karen McCarthy Woolf was in Clapham Library, south London; and Clare Shaw led her workshops in Manchester Central Library. Our local library partners did everything they could to drum up fresh poet-punters – and most of our workshops were packed with people, almost all of whom were new to Clare, if not all of them quite new to poetry (as you will see from the brief biographies at the foot of each poem). Many (but not all!) of our poet-participants stuck the course: and the bulk of the poems in this book are edited versions of their workshopped poems. The poet-tutors edited these poems as you see them here. At one point, a participant asked if there were any decent audio recordings of Clare's poetry. And there were none – so actor Toby Jones agreed to record a selection of poems and prose extracts – by way of supporting our workshops' study and enjoyment of Clare. These recording are free to all via the project website, address below.

The second part of the project was the product of my increasing obsession – mentioned above, and much of it detailed in my book on Clare[4] – with the fact that the first poem in Clare's first book was picked up, set to original music, and performed in an opera just one month after the book was published – and at the Royal Theatre Drury Lane no less. This poem – 'The Meeting' – was then set to other musical pieces – old standards and new compositions – and across the nineteenth century was to become a regular feature of music-hall performances across Britain – and a staple of musical tuition books, songsters and compilations. Indeed it even went so far as to become a standard ballad in the United States. So common was it that novelists and playwrights referred to the well-known ditty, relying on the fact that their audience would know the tune and the words. And, typical of his luck, Clare did not know of this success *at all*: he didn't make a penny out of it, and he never knew that long before he died, this early, simple love song was in the common air, everywhere, in the English-speaking world. And right at the start

Detail, playbill advertising shows at the Theatre Royal, Drury Lane, for Saturday, 19 February 1820.

of his literary 'career', he missed Madame Vestris's performance of his song in the opera *The Siege of Belgrade* in February 1820 (he arrived in London for his first visit, the following month). She played a peasant girl Lilla, and she sang the peasant poet's new song. Clare was thrilled about it – 'I was uncommonly pleased at the circumstance' he wrote.[5] It would have confirmed that in early 1820, everything looked pretty good for his prospects. A major, trendy London publisher had pushed his first book well – and the reviews were mostly happy – the book going to four editions in that first year. The 'peasant poet' was flavour of the month – albeit for not for long. But still, in that first year, with good reason, Clare could look forward to lifting his family out of the abject poverty into which he had been born. Patrons came forward, generously, with money and books and unwanted advice; exciting literary connections were established; and new, meaningful friendships were made, with all manner of cultured and intellectually-energising people. Clare was disappointed with the muddy strip of the Thames, but there is no question he was excited by what London uniquely had to offer. In 1822 he wrote to his publisher: 'I wish I livd nearer you at least I wish London w[oud] creep within 20 miles of helpstone'.[6] He loved his home village of Helpston; but he loved London too. Sometimes, he felt very cut off. He wanted it all, and for a while it looked like he might do really well.

Was there any other major Romantic poet who played the fiddle and read and wrote musical notation? Clare was a music-reader and a fiddle player. He is a thoroughly musical poet: music had a hugely formative impact on his verse. But I don't read music, which means that all of my study of this poem-cum-song, 'The Meeting', was carried out in musical silence; even as I looked at songsters and chapbooks and songsheets and textbooks with score after musical score giving this poem tuneful life, I just could not hear it. What I wanted to do, was dramatize Clare 'meeting' his own poem, on stage. I wanted to correct that big missed opportunity of early 1820 and enable Clare (well, our version of him at least) to hear his own poem transformed by song, for the first time. And the plan was to do that in 2020, the 200th anniversary year of his first book being published, and of his first song being sung on a London stage: the 'peasant poet' in an opera! It would be a remarkable 'meeting' of cultures, of styles, of rural and urban, of peasant poetry and operatic staging, and of Clare's past with our present moment. This second part of our project would see Clare's poetry come together with music again, only this time with new contemporary compositions alongside the old, on the London stage again, with actor Toby Jones (who has played Clare before in the 2015 feature film *By Our Selves* and who is a lifelong lover of his work) as Clare.

In 2019 in St Botolph's Church, in Helpston, at the John Clare Society festival on Clare's birthday, 13 July, I was lucky to meet celebrated composer Julian Philips. Julian had been studying Clare and setting his poems to his own compositions for many years. He had long nursed a desire to do something bigger, grander, for the stage. And so the project's second part began to take shape. With musician, writer and producer Kate Romano, playwright and librettist Stephen Plaice, and with Julian's compositions – and then with Arts Council England's project grant along with significant backing from Oxford Brookes University and the John Clare Society, we were heading for a full stage performance. Julian Philips, Kate Romano, Toby Jones and I enjoyed a warm-up public event at Oxford Brookes in February 2020, which was the first time I heard an opera singer – the brilliant William Searle – perform 'The Meeting' – and it was a very moving evening. All was then set for the performance at the musical venue Bush Hall in west London, booked for the 26 April 2020 – two hundred years and a month, after Clare first arrived in the capital. Tickets started to sell, but then – well, we all know what happened then. Among the myriad disappointments of 2020, our show had to be postponed. At the time of writing, we still intend to put on that show, but when we do not know.

Our project of two parts comes together, and to partial fruition, with this book. Our poet tutors have written a poem each, responding to Clare; and they edited their participants' poems, which form the bulk of this book. Stephen Plaice has generously extracted his work-in-progress *The Fallen Elm* – his title for the stage show, taken from the title of one of Clare's most celebrated poems. And Julian Philips has written an essay about composing in response to Clare, and offers us one of his works here, again published for the first time.

The Meeting: www.brookes.ac.uk/the-meeting

NOTES

1   For the best account of Clare's psychological weather, see Jonathan Bate, *John Clare: A Biography* (London: Picadord, 2003), pp. 421–529.

2   'The Lament of Swordy Well', in *John Clare: Major Works*, ed. by Eric Robinson and David Powell (Oxford: Oxford World's Classics, 2004), pp. 148–9, ll. 57–64 and 81–8.

3   *John Clare By Himself*, ed. by Eric Robinson and David Powell (Ashington and Manchester: MidNAG/Carcanet, 1996), p. 233.

4   Simon Kövesi, *John Clare: Nature, Criticism and History* (London: Palgrave Macmillan, 2017). See especially pp. 52–61.

5   *John Clare By Himself*, p. 136.

6   To John Taylor, 8 February 1822, *The Letters of John Clare*, ed. by Mark Storey (Oxford: Clarendon Press, 1985), pp. 229–30 (p. 230).

Poems from Bradford and Keighley Libraries
EDITED BY SARAH CORBETT

Musing in Bradford's City Park

Melissa Dennison

Warm day sitting by the Pavilion Café
Watching people lost in conversation
Finding solace in the shade
Time just seems to slip away

No need for coffee, no need for tea
A wave of human voices, and laughter
From children as they play
In and around the fountains

People in ceaseless motion
Milling, rushing or sitting on the deck
Talking, giggling, hooting and yelling
As they lark in the spray

A sea of colour sparkles, dances, shimmers
Dazzles – vibrant reds, joyous oranges, laid back blues
I try to differentiate these colours
But they refuse

The staff from the café hurry past
Sound engulfs me, crashes in my ears
Then suddenly retreats like a tide
My friend and I look at one another and smile

'Time for tea?' I say
Time like water runs through my fingers
Slipping and flowing away

I have a longstanding love affair with words. I often lose myself in books, stories and poems and I have written stories and poems since being a child. For me words are like oxygen – indispensable. Writing is simply part of my being, my becoming, of who and what I am.

Broken

Julie Darling

Thunder rocked the valley in the night,
Lightning shocked the dark,
A tongue of fire seared your heart

And hurled you to the ground.

Your limbs lie broken,
Your blossom crushed confetti,
Your fractured nub a shocking white

Against the rain-black bark,
Untainted heartwood, source of life,
Exposed, unguarded, pure.

I touch you there, stroke jagged flesh,
Press my face to rain-soaked skin

And mourn.

Words arrive, unbidden,
A prayer for healing,
For your heart's wounding.

On this quiet morning, green and grievous,

We hold each other,
Rock gently in the wind.

Julie Darling is a poet, musician, artist and teacher. Best known for atmospheric performance of her poetry with Celtic harp accompaniment, her work draws on her intimate relationship with nature and explores the spiritual legacy of her Celtic ancestors. Based in Yorkshire she has performed in the UK and USA, and leads retreats in wild places, such as the Isle of Iona.

Playing Out

Patricia Henny

We went to rec to play,
hillocks and rough ground
up and down,
we'd slide on our coats,
tumbling one on top of t'other
legs green with grass sap.
Such stalks there were,
green of course, but
black and red and brown,
some wi' nobbles
that if you pushed up from below
would rush to the top and
burst out.
The red ones fooled our eyes
and mixed us up
thinking they were some other
thing than grass.
Shiny buttercup mirrors
held under our chins,
daisies threaded into crowns,
celandines to burnish up our frocks,
endless quests for four-leaved clover
to bring us luck.
A gang of boys spoilt our play
turned it into danger dares
wi' their loud voices
and mocking laughs,
rough hands pushing, pulling
until we ran
back to rows of streets.
A cobbler's mucky leather shop,
a butcher bashing at murdered meat,
women coughing dust from beaten rugs
chip scrap batter stinking the air.

I started writing poetry at school and continued on into my early twenties. I went
on to develop my interest in theatre as an amateur performer and director, studied
voice with a private tutor and took my Guildhall and LLAMDA exams and this
reignited my love of poetry.

Beech Tree
after 'To a Fallen Elm'

Jill Lang

Our hide-and-seek secret garden beech
A giant on elephant feet
Svelte, skin smooth and cool to the touch
Whose lime leaves unfurled, rippled in the breeze
And sang lullabies fit for Sirens,
Whose nuts like fire crackers fell
Crunched, popped, pricked naked feet,
Branches rocking the swing like a cradle.
Visited less but always loved, girth thickened,
Limbs creaking, storm weary, still singing
For the gift of a new generation.

Retired now after working in publishing, as a French teacher and bringing up two
sons, Jill is pursuing her interest in creative writing. Scrabble games with her
father, a passion for letter writing shared with her grandmother, two inspirational
foreign language teachers gave her a lifelong passion for words.

Horizons

Claire Shepherd

There was a time when horizons were small,
One house, two neighbours, two schools,
Friends from childhood through teenage years,
One garden explored from corner to corner
And walks over well-trodden routes
After Sunday School and Sunday roast.

At home, belonging yet burning for cultures
Encountered in novels or textbooks,
At last, University, opportunities for travel,
Trains, flights, ferries, multitudinous time zones,
New friends and far-flung languages,
An extended family understood through
Signs and gestures; then, our children, a blend.

Now, I kneel in prayer in a mosque not a church
And my old garden is viewed in photographs
Or glimpsed on Skype in the background
Yet in my mind I explore that garden from corner to corner,
Follow that Sunday path after Sunday School
And Sunday roast, recapture old horizons.

Born and bred in rural Oxfordshire in the 1970s, I enjoyed a childhood spent largely outside, exploring the countryside. As an adult I travelled for study, and then lived and worked in the Middle East before moving to Keighley in 2015. I embraced the Muslim faith a few years ago.

Parkwood

Linda Tugwell

Ancient wood on leaf-green hill
Between urban boxes and blackened school
Dog walkers on mossy cobbles
Grass that never knew a scythe
Canopy of oak, elm and ash
Wild deer kept from prying eyes
Hidden under dappled sun skies

From a raddle-stained bench
A rotten branch worships the beck
Wild flowers poking through gaps
Silence shattered by rambling children
Lighting campfires in the precious copse
Tiny hands hugging gathered twigs
Treasured skills that are never lost

I am seventy years old and only started writing poetry about four years ago. My poetry is focused on family, people and nature. I love John Clare as he reflects the themes of his time and locality but it still so contemporary and relevant today.

Cowslips in Sudbury

Brenda Watts

Cowslips grow here my sister said
Away from the busy road
Come and see, and we were led
To where we did not know

Up the verge into a grassy field
Little shuffles over grass until a dip
Revealed sweet peeping cowslips
Yellow shy, the hiding grass between

Away from cows and treading feet.
Together in the small glade
Little fingers moved blades of grass
To see more yellow maids

Perk their pretty springing heads
Now wishing to be seen.

Brenda Watts lived in Sudbury for a time as a young girl, where her father worked in local farm, and has lived in Buttershaw, Bradford, for many years. She has wonderful memories of her rural childhood. 'We'd look at the threshing going on in a field when we played through the tall hawthorn hedge taking Dad his snap, tea in a metal can, and bread.'

Birch Tree on Haworth Moor
after 'To a Fallen Elm'

Christina Wilson

I drop weary
by the river
under your silver bark
fingers tracing
your cracked body,
listen to your breath
in the spaces
between bracken and moss,
your twisted roots
spiraling and long
gripping the moor.
You remember the storm,
fury of rocks cascading,
stone bridge tumbling
downstream,
watched it fall,
your back bent
into the wind.
Your roots dug deeper
and you stretched sideways,
your trunk growing
and splintering
as you aged,
your scars shimmering.

Christina lives in West Yorkshire. She enjoys the feeling of a pen moving on paper and the warmth of books. Christina has an MA in Creative Writing and celebrates the therapeutic benefits of writing, working to share the benefits of writing and creativity in her facilitation of therapeutic writing workshops.

here song

Sarah Corbett

i am the red tree, exploding eternally
in me the sap leaps, germinating song

i am the oak, here two hundred a thousand years
my voice when the wind withers through me

here where we have always been –
the hare in the fold of grass, the grouse
in her nest in the hollow among the stones

we are the stones, speaking stonily
an aeon of assonance, a slow dance
of shimmy & settlement

we are the rocks, cupped & ringing
the lichens who whiten into language

we are the snails who love the trees
wrapping our feet along the branches
we the slugs, the red winged beetles

we the spiders the knitters & weavers
multiple & various, the telepathic listeners

& under the earth a muttering
of worm & water, of seethe & moan
suck & split, seed's plink, puck

here where light drops into the field
where mist rises in loops & waves
& winter becomes us

Sarah Corbett is a poet, emerging novelist and tutor. She's published five collections of poetry, most recently, *A Perfect Mirror* (pavilion Poetry/Liverpool University Press, 2018), which contains a number of poems that respond directly to Clare. She lives in West Yorkshire and teaches Creative Writing for Lancaster University.

Poems from Peterborough Central Library
EDITED BY JOHN GALLAS

4 poems from Nature

Jax Hives

I
a winter hedge with wrens in it

The hedge gapped and thin
Woven with the smallest birds
Safety sure in barbs

II
a gnarled pollarded willow with a heron amongst the branches

The stars looked on us
Pollarded willow by water
Heron waits for fish

III
the View Across

Autumn oaks
Great lofty wooden tops
Thunder as storms play

And water in the ruts of cultivated fields
Sits reflecting
As the veil of fog reveals the day

IV
the Hedgerow

How do you think it feels to have discarded items thrown at you
By arms flailing from passing cars.
Raining discarded disposable cardboard coffee cups,

And the rest.
A reaction I get from just being so beautiful
that people cannot cope.
Perverse it may seem, just like them.

When I am woven I look so tidy and severe but it helps me do my job
As housing officer to many, even when the
Cutting begins: when my babies have left I still do my job.

Jax Hives: Writing and drawing are part of my creative process, responding to the environment, making sense of my surroundings, utilising visual and spoken language. Empty pages are my laboratory where I can interpret man's 'footprint', the ambivalent relationship and impact on the environment. Exploring abstract ideas, structured and disordered forms, patterns and shapes produced by man and nature; divisions, intersections and the spaces we create.

A poem fell on me

Linda Anderson

I nearly didn't go.
It was an outdoor performance and the play's title rankled:
The Long Life and Great Good Fortune of John Clare.
I saw myself shivering in the nippy autumn cool,
enduring some upbeat take on trauma.
My village is next to yours,
the place where the wrong wife came to fetch you
home in a cart
after your long hike from the asylum,
surviving on grass, sleeping in ditches.

The day turned out bright and warm,
'More sweet than Summer in her loveliest hours', as you would say.
We gathered in the courtyard at Helpston, seated around your statue.
I was two rows behind you
Sensing your force field.
A huge mind, yes, enclosed in that tiny, toiling body;
A reminder of hunger, all kinds of stunting.

We were close to the actors and the rest of the audience;
two dramas to behold.
Opposite me, a man nodded off.
I tried to avoid the stare of a fierce-eyed woman.
There was a man with a rapt, stricken face
as heart-hitting as the play.

At the end the poet flung his poems in the air,
a blizzard of giant confetti.
A poem fell on me, flittered off my head and into my lap.
Handwritten, on parchment-like paper, crinkled.
I slid it into my bag, unfolded
and walked away, anointed.

Note: 'The Long Life and Great Good Fortune of John Clare' by Tony Ramsay
was performed at the Clare Cottage, Helpston by Eastern Angles in September
2012. The quoted line is from Clare's sonnet 'To Autumn'.

Linda Anderson writes mainly fiction and non-fiction. She is co-editor of *Female Lines: New Writing by Women from Northern Ireland* (New Island, 2017). Her novel *Cuckoo,* originally published by The Bodley Head, was reissued by Turnpike Books in 2018.

I am a spider…

Clare Currie

I am a spider playing pizzicato on the strings
that fasten bold upon the oak's firm frame.
Above, leaves silhouette the waning sky
and shudder as I hear his tread again.
A figure bent on other-worldly things,
with Mary on his lips and through his brow,
catches look of hornbeam, hazel, wren, then
stops and stoops at cowslips now and now.

Clare Currie was Peterborough Poet Laureate 2017–19. Her work ranges from facilitating workshops to performing and writing for the stage. She has written pieces for Eastern Angles and Jumped Up Theatre. Clare was awarded Arts Council DYCP funding to work on her solo theatre piece 'Cold Snap', which centres on being a sports woman and a mother.

The Dawn Chorus

Cazz Anders

A 'best-time-of-the-day'-er,
I creep from the house as
daybreak pushes stealthy fingers into
puddles of dewy darkness.
Night-tightened leaves unfurl
like a groom to his lover's caress
and sloes' cataract bloom
glows in rose-hazed dawn.
Through hedgerows,
sunlight saturated,
I am drenched in
the ritual aubade.

I'm a (very) mature Creative writing student at De Montfort university but
live close to Helpston, and have always loved John Clare's work, which seems
deceptively uncomplicated. As I am a prose writer, the amazing poetry workshop
cemented my belief that producing 'effortless' poetry is exceptionally hard work!

Three Days

Alison Fure

Our forest network of downy threads
Are compacted by your feet.
Ouch, we are constricted by
the weight of your heavy clouds.

Fungus gnats scatter as you approach
and save us from the hole-makers.
As stillness returns, they lay eggs
and larvae consume us into doilies

Adult gnats exit after three days
Food for Autumn's night-sniffing bats.
Sun rise and we are deliquescing
you linger on stone-heaps, between homes.

Alison Fure has spent 22 years working as an ecologist informing land managers
of the wildlife interest on their holdings; she enjoys curating wonderful walks
for the public from wildlife, wassails and more recently, Soundwalks. She writes
nature blogs and chap books including Kingston's Apple Story.

Two Helpston haikus

Sharon Mather

venerable tree
ancient raven keeping watch
forest now a copse

days of our childhood
fly quick on kingfisher's wings
days are blue and cold

Destroying Beauty

Kate Caoimhe Arthur

Horizons draw in closer this time of year
fog's outbreath picks out the water tower

the poplars, church spire, a house or two
a pair of whoopers write a secret code

above the field sprayed with glyphosate
gorgeous as an illuminated manuscript

amber, umber, and searing gold strokes
outlined in peacock-black and shot with lime green

what small creature would be scared from her home here
babies sucking at her teats as she runs for cover

the other way a field with the skin ripped off
dark wave upon wave of torn muscle

the blackbird flock curls away, a single egret rises
colourless and solitary in the velvet sky

rain through exhaust fumes as a car lurches past
heaven gleams in the puddle it splashed.

Kate Caoimhe Arthur was born in Bangor and lives now in the Cambridgeshire
Fens. In 2017 she became the Fenland Poet Laureate. In 2018 she was selected for
Poetry Ireland Introductions. She collaborates with the fine-art printmaker Iona
Howard and is working on a pamphlet of Fen-based poems.

Haiku for John Clare

Arthur Chapman

The dykes are brimming,
overboiling, bubbling up,
spilling the land flat.

*

Magpies on the moor:
wimple-wearers gossiping;
silent-movie song.

*

Rampant stag-beetle:
alphamale, alphabeetle,
lettering the wood.

Arthur Chapman is a history educator and education researcher at University College London. He lives in Peterborough. He blogs poetry occasionally at www.themeasurementofflatness.wordpress.com.

Forget Me Not

Hannah Chapman

I am a blooming flower blowing in the breeze.
Surrounded by trees and others like me,
Almost identical.

I am moving gently from side to side,
As the wind pushes me.
Looking up at the red sky.
Swaying from side to side.
The wind blowing me.

As evening's light pierces through the trees,
I hear the leaves crunching.

The sound of footsteps getting closer.
I wonder who it can be?

I look up at the John Clare, so close I can hear him breathe

I sigh to see him go.

I enjoyed the company.

Hannah Chapman was born in Kingston-upon-Thames and has lived in
Cornwall, Cumbria and Cambridgeshire. She volunteers at Flag Fen and
Peterborough Museum. She is currently studying History, English, Psychology,
Philosophy and Sociology. She has spent time in Japan and wants to go back.

We Are Reed
(a mile north-east from Helpston)

Kathryn Parsons

We are Reed.
Upright, tall,
Feet grounded in soft silt mud.
Family clustered tight around
We sing our evening whisper-song.

Above, the starlings gather,
Chatter-dancing
          rustle-whirling
                    cloud-up down

                         settle

                         lift

                         return.

We are their safe bed roost.

I live just a few miles from John Clare's Helpston home and often walk in his footsteps. I am a mixed media artist and visual storyteller. From porcelain plants to eco-printed poems, I create intricate hand-modelled sculptures that weave together tales of people, places and the natural world. Writing poetry is new for me.

woodmouse encounters the sole of john clare

Rennie Parker

sometimes   as   then

dunno   *brown*   and

feet   nose   feetnose   oh

and   tail-wire

crunchycrunchycrunchycrunchy   and

        stop

here   and   there

here   andthere

beady sees   BIG

what?   only green   until grey

......tremor! ground! shake!   *dum dum*

me down

        fur-stiff

           ears out

brown hard beast many-eyes no-mouth

        stop

call   a lowing   *'o hooooooo'*

roll   it   me....... nut! cob!

he pass   god of cob

roll on

me   push   light-dawn-black

crackle   into   crack

slidey round

       to sleep

Rennie Parker is a poet based in Lincolnshire, published by Shoestring Press; her previous collection was *The Complete Electric Artisan* (2017). Between 2010 and 2014 she worked as an education officer at John Clare's restored cottage. A woodmouse lived in the '19th century herb garden', observed by staff.

Heron

Hilary Jay

Laser-eyed tether
sunset silhouette
red pierced visceral
fish eye glint reflects
rippled eddy mirror

Hilary Jay is a Visual Communications Tutor, an East Anglian 'Open Skies' /
Elemental Arts Naturalist, recording Macro studies of wildlife, fossil & stone
fossicker (e.g. a Lithic blade gleaned in Helpston) and Senior Photo-journalist BIPP
(Print Press), Lincoln RAF. Teacher Trained, and studied at Nottingham University,
and Cambridge University CEI. Creative Writing in 'New Perspectives'.

JC knew of a climatic change

Gary Huskisson

Fields were the essence of its song
John Clare wrote the tweets of the birdsong
He knew
That only the Sparrows will remember the chorus
As the landowners go bust
He knew
That his Field of words would turn into Field of woes
That the sowing of seeds would grow into seducing souls
JC knew
Where once he languished for hours
You can smell in winter, summer flowers!
He knew
That there would be barking up the wrong tree
As the butterfly would stay the same as a Bee
Only to be seen on silent TV
With subliminal messages from Aldi
That it is only gluten that can roam free
JC knew
That pesticides and sprays
Would implant the pitchforks in the hay
While day trippers would bury their waste
Then go away

He knew
That after Capability Brown's Burghley culling
Life would never be endearing
There be no more larking about
The petals are blooming in, not out
JC knew
The day will come
When the bees work for minimum wage
This is the butterfly effect
Of Climate Change.
Who knew
That summertime pleasures
Would be the hunt for a caterpillar
In record breaking adverse weather
Living across the tracks causes clut, clut clutter
We knew
Locking up JC was not mad
It was just sad

I am Gary Huskisson, a proud Peterborian, but in spitting distance of John
Clare's Glinton Spire. A trained Storyteller who discovered poetry – and John
Clare. Currently undertaking an oral history project called PeterStory which has
served to enrich my interest in the Helpston Poet.

John Clare's Muse is a Tree

Nicole Reilly

Jack Frost's evening is minutes from dusk
and I stand amongst brittle branches and browned leaves,
missing a tomboy's trainers.
Our sky is littered with jaded beaks and I smell a mossy stench.

A melancholic man in leather boots approaches my field again.
He scrutinises my architecture, my body of bark and puts me in a poem -
birds stop singing: we all flatline until
he vanishes into the urban streets beside us, with his inkless pen.

Before attending the workshop last summer, I knew very little of John Clare
but as a third-year English student at De Montfort University, my interests in
literature expand way beyond what I'm familiar with. I've been reading and
writing poetry for some years, my favourite poet being Emily Brontë.

John Clare is Approaching

Ann Marshall

I am a hungry, bristly badger
Emerging from my leafy sett,
Hesitant and snuffling the night air.
Moonlight filters through the branches,

Twigs snap and there is rustling -
Who approaches? Keep still and flatten.
Shuffling fades and, free to start my search,
I trundle out into the gloom.

I live in Lincolnshire and am semi-retired as a writer, editor and proof reader. I
studied Humanities at Nottingham Trent University as a mature student. I was
fortunate enough to study John Clare with Professor John Goodridge. I joined
the John Clare Society on leaving University, and have been part of the group
organising the annual Festival in Helpston for many years. I am the Society's
Publicity Officer and love meeting Clare devotees in that role.

John Clare's 3D Printer

Pete Cardinal Cox

I would have a craftsman make
A book entitled in gold
All That Is Yet Unwritten
That opens to reveal
A tiny globe of the Earth
Such as my schoolmaster had
That opens to reveal
The wild dog rose in bud
Twist of the stem brings to bloom
That opens to reveal
My wives Mary and Patty
Combined into one sweet girl
That opens to reveal
Her true heart from out her soul
My name engraved upon it
That opens to reveal
A bird's nest, twigs and feathers
Small hen bird upon her egg
That opens to reveal
My sister, these long years gone
Grown to womanhood, her arms
Open to welcome me home

Former Poet Laureate of Peterborough (2003) and winner of the John Clare
Trust Poetry Prize (2009), Pete Cardinal Cox has toured his one-man show *High
Stakes* as far as Helsinki and Dublin.

Group Poem on a Museum Object – an 18th-century Yoke

Peterborough Workshop

T oil-tethered, trudging

H eavy-harnessed through the mud,

E die shoulders the swedes towards the

Y ard. Scud-clouds glower,

O verloaded; the pigs jostle and

K ick. *Late, I can lay down.*

E ach step again … again …

Group Poem on a Museum Object –
18th-century Yoke

Peterborough Workshop

T rembling task-master,

H eavy-hauled collar-bone,

E ases the bucket-bearer,

Y oung-frame toiling and bound.

O vercast, cloud-pressed,

K eening pails shimmer and quiver.

E vening weight.

Group Poem on a Museum Object –
18th-Century Pitchfork

Peterborough Workshop

P okey-hook harvest-help,

I nstrument of blisters, blood and

T oil. Iron-horned, a

C ow's-head tuned for tossing.

H aymakers stacking stooks,

F odder-pressing, golden-gather,

O at, barley, corn, rye, hop and bean.

R eturned to hedge-rest, end of day,

K ite-spied, snail-silvered, moon-watched.

Mr Clare's 2020 vision: attack of the Inscape

John Gallas

I went for a walk. The old canal.
The mudded towpath. Bleariness above.
Chance of rain. The long duck-runway
metalled-grey between crook-ivied oaks
and holly-furze, all still
as writings on the air.

No Tyke, no Thomas, no pitch, no pipe,
no hums, no hahs, no careful of this,
no heedless of that - just me,
a toyless soft machine
shovelled out of practicals and musement,
and passed along, expugnable as jelly.

The world rolled by, leaf, stock and stone,
a bobbed-wire tunnel of amaze,
each root and thorn an ecstasy,
each ripple cutting at my quick,
each weed a wound of what it was,
in my unarmoured self.

I took my scourge in quiet part.
My blood was moved. I gushed like saints.
A trinity of ducks skidded
scalpel-keen down to the water.
Oak and holly caught eye-fire.
I got to Spicers Bridge, and went no more.

And in my quiet house the small white walls
applied like bandages the salve of common ways,
returning to my too-flayed heart
a kinder kind of swell, and company.
The sky was grey. I took a pipe; and nursed
the precious scab of my poor self, inside my chair.

John Gallas: En Zed poet, published by Carcanet (www.carcanet.co.uk).
More info at www.johngallaspoetry.co.uk

Poems from Clapham Library
Edited by Karen McCarthy Woolf

The Dead Sheep

Balaka Fell-Holden

There! On yonder lower field, a sheep lies dead
See, its face is fallen– its burst-through tongue a purple-red.
Baking on a sea of emerald-green it did once eat
Each blade cropped circle-slow as if a dainty treat.
Now busy flies dive on senseless eyes from giddy height
While the nesting-rook aloft covets the fleece still bright
Who'll this sheepish mound some kind words give 'ere it's heaven-sent?
Whose forlorn cheeks will the bugle blow as in times ancient?
For the poet's inkwell's dry and her rhyming lines all spent.

Hark! The tuneful lark sends forth a fond farewell
And unites with nature's choir its joyful memories to tell.
The swallow swoops in low salute under a vaulted blue-lit sky
And the curlew's chirrup more reach has than a preacher's cry.
The plover lifts its bustling skirts and bolts from mossy trees
As if late to this new-found church and startles the owl that flees.
The nimble mice and grasshoppers form the congregation
And o'er the woolly head the daisies nod in sweet devotion,
For no more the shepherd's call can rouse, nor join this lamentation.

Balaka Fell-Holden has two grown up children and works in a library in East London. Her hobbies include swimming, cooking and photography. She loves watching films, especially from the 1970s.

Clare Diary Redacted Through a Midday Sieve

Cath Drake

I employ the woodpecker, passing clowns and
the opening of a rude bridge
on my feelings.
The gipseys hear
the restless song sweet jug.
I pulld my hat over my eyes
to hang in summer sky,
often lingerd in raptures
in wild marshy fen.
I wandered thymy mole hill, ripening hay
with scarlet head aches, troubling dragon flyes,
making the whispering wind
play humble horse bee, and muttered
to the leaves
of the wanton green chattering morning
with brown mossy crowns
idly peeping round the orison's circle.

An Australian who lives in London, Cath Drake has published poems in anthologies and literary magazines in Australia, the UK and US, and performs her work widely. She has been short-listed for the Venture Poetry Prize and the Manchester Poetry Prize and was second in the 2017 Resurgence Poetry School eco-poetry prize, and highly commended in the latter in 2019. *Sleeping with Rivers* won a Mslexia/Seren poetry pamphlet prize and was a Poetry Book Society Choice. *The Shaking City,* her first full collection, is out in 2020 with Seren Books. www.cathdrake.com

Enclosure

Charlotte Mackie

'Inclosure came and trampled on the grave
Of labour's rights and left the poor a slave'
– John Clare

Then enclosure came
I used to graze me sheep on t' land. They 'ad room to roam, now…common land? What common land?

Then enclosure came
I would see me family every Sunday, It was a fair way, but I'm spry. Now, I work in t' big house all week, and only visit them on holidays a few times a year. So many fences blocking paths we're forbidden to cross, what took me a few hours, takes much of a day…

Then enclosure came
I'd a selion of land in the open field. I grew wheat. Once I grew barley. I remember me sheep. Today I have nothing. Common land? Small. Every man grazes their animals on it, no grass left to eat …

Then enclosure came
The land I love to roam? Some days I go on a trespass, climb over the high fence and walk everywhere like I did as a boy. I watch out for man traps, mind, can take your leg off. And always I feel I'm doing something wrong…

Then enclosure came
The land has been stolen from me. That marsh where I once saw a will-o-the-wisp. Ah, I remember it was Autumn… evening. Now – fenced and drained.

Gone.

Charlotte Mackie has recently retired from a career in teaching, so now has time to perfect her poetry. A proud mother of two grown-up children, and an equally proud grandmother, retirement has given her the time to start a community poetry group. She believes sharing one's poetry, without judgement or scrutiny, increases confidence and well being. She has also recently become Brixton & Streatham Stanza rep (meaning she is the area contact for members of The Poetry Society).

Ninth Night of the Last Slave

Jenny Mitchell

On a narrow bed, she raised her arms
twigs of a rotting tree – creaked
I have not been born.

Her hands waved in the air, dry leaves.
Since reaching out for Momma
I was trapped in cane.
No time to make these flowers grow.

The bed shone as she gave off light.
Soil was dark again.
This heart – she pointed at the withered trunk
could not bear fruit.

Master would have stolen from the first.
My womb was forced
to make a path of red hibiscus.

Here she moaned
sound of a distant breeze
deep in her throat.
I longed to go to God,
sink in a stream above my head.

These legs –
she pointed at thin roots
knew He was only dirt
piled in a mighty heap.

She reached up
to the highest branches
snagged like hair
pulled out a wisp

of hummingbird
its song a stroking hand
the awe of wings
a fan above her face.

She settled in the resting place
closed her seed-like eyes
began again.

Jenny Mitchell is joint winner of the annual Geoff Stevens' Memorial Poetry Prize and a finalist in the Fool for Poetry International Chapbook competition. Her work has been broadcast on Radio 4 and BBC 2, and published in *Rialto, New European, Interpreter's House*; and translated into Italian in *Versodove*. A debut collection, *Her Lost Language*, published by Indigo Dreams, was the Poetry Kit Book of the Month for November 2019.

Bee Elegy

Julian Bishop

a dead bee in the street, the second one
I've seen in three days: roadside flotsam
chased across the pavement in the breeze

now a bobble of fuzz lodged in the gutter
tucked among stained cigarette butts,
a blackened cotton bud, plastic wrappers.

I pick it up by the wing, worried it might
sting – but it's a thistle seed of bee,
dusted tremble of fur stirring in the dirt.

I place the remains under a tree, temporary
headstone, body of soot, dead yellow flame,
wisps of wing clinging to tarmac and ash.

Julian Bishop is a former television journalist living in North London who is working on his first pamphlet. He was runner-up in the 2018 International Ginkgo Prize for Eco Poetry and shortlisted for the Bridport Poetry Prize in the previous year. He is a member of several London Stanza groups and runs a regular contemporary poetry workshop in Enfield.

Crowded Places

Rachel Woolf

'Crowded places, I shunned them as noises too rude and fled to …
where the flower in green darkness buds, blossoms and fades'

[from 'Song' by John Clare]

As I move towards the door of the train
NEXT STATION: CLAPHAM JUNCTION
I spy a wee dog, a doggie dog

Its doggie-ness stands out in a carriage of folk
though the stand-out dog isn't actually standing
but rather is sat on the lap of a chap who wears a T-shirt
which bears a block of upper-case letters, I scan in an instant

WILD ISLAND
OF COLONSAY

Just fancy!

I tippy-tongue make to chat to the chap upon whose lap
the dog is sat about this chip of the Hebrides
but hesitate and just exchange usual pleasantries
with the dog, which licks me. I like that

Yet yon wild island siren-sings and at Platform 2
I fail to board the Overground bound for Clapham High Street
and its spiral library, stepping instead
upon the deck of a CalMac ferry

This Lammastide evening, surfing without getting wet
I find WILD ISLAND is a brand of GIN
with the ISLE OF COLONSAY the site of its distillery

Aw jings! But listen here!
'Six hand-gathered native plants' labelled as botanicals
provide, no less, 'its heart and soul'

bog myrtle / meadowsweet / lemon balm
wild water mint / sea buckthorn / heather flowers

Buds & blossoms! Buds & blossoms!
The poesy of marketing

Rachel Woolf is from the Firth of Forth and writes for pleasure in both Scots and English. Her poems have been placed in competitions and published in anthologies in Scotland, Ireland and Cornwall. The dialect elements of John Clare's work hold particular appeal.

Seeing Keeps Me Wild

Rebecca Patenon

Urban life   Rural life   Tower living   Hut living
City or Landscape   Imaginary or Real,
always known to me, yet to a twelve to sixteen-
line song I have never cut my Ideal
or perhaps through a passage for fun
as one takes a moody turn
into a medieval alley cobbled
after Blackfriars Bridge slope.

Tho' I have reshaped the world
round a drafted beer, never was I able to drop
the city and adopt the country.
I am the shrub outside my window,
in how its branches twine round the lamp post
and conceal the sign of the parking hours,
in how its green espouses the metal charcoal-coloured.

It is the joy of nature's reclaim, the mind of the poet;
a withdrawn existence to reach in my soul
and lean into seeing the present above all.
Cat fights do the trick of awe, as they joust
in my garden, under a sycamore young,
for the top vista on a tower of slabs
where the winner, stretched fully, takes a nap,
and dreams … dreams … of convoys of glee.

Rebecca Patenon is an adventurer in writing. When she is not exploring the craft, she watches films, savours world food and argues with her friends at The Railway. She is currently working on a play.

Self-Portrait (London, 2019)

Saralara

I am – yet what I am is only behind the bright screen.
I lie to my colleagues about where I come from
    afraid of stabbing my heels on the velvet carpet
        leaving marks (for every exit wound).

Into the nothingness, I swim.
Over five days in the dark sea
losing some parts of me.
On the fifth day, I breath
unable to feel   some parts of me.

Some parts of me are
      no longer   there.

They say go home. 'Home': a sudden bit of memory:
home is where the bills are
the lamps with the melted bulbs
the rotten onion at the bottom of the cabinet
              the cold.

I long for crossing the threshold
from the ordinary world towards
the broken screen, on the floor
where a dancer could not get home because she got stranded in paradise.
(Where I choose to say paradise).
Where I toast with my friends – at 7 am – for every exit wound.

I can feel my torso
my hair combed towards the blue by galaxy dust
every tiny asteroid.

In the deepest part of the high, I extend my arms until my fingertips dilate
the Universe's cervix: I'm here, dancing
alone: everyone else is inside me.

Saralara is a queer Spanish millennial who migrated to London seven years ago. Saralara's poetry digs into the meanings of femininity and sexuality, as well as existential pain. Her writings have been published in *La Rabia del Axolotl, MAI: feminism & visual culture, and the collective book Alright Britain.* Saralara has recently performed at the European Poetry Festival and the Wilderness Event at the Poetry Society in London.

Still Life of a Township (Zuihitsu)

Thembe Mvula

Things that are near yet far
lampposts ascend along steep streets, watch over us
like towering guardians. from brick house and broad drives
to mud walls and corrugated iron
crossing e street felt like time travel

Things that are far yet near
here where soul doesn't slumber, at night
boisterous beats bounce from local taverns,
taxi speakers spill kwaito into the ears of pedestrians,
we inhale and exhale music

On a bright moonlit night
streetlights replace voices of relatives
and usher me back into the house,
how i envy the dogs that howl
through the night, taking full reign of the streets

Things of elegant beauty
after the cocks crow bhuti washes his second car
on the side of the road, tosses a bucket over the bonnet
and foamy water flows downhill into a sort of drain-
water stains form foggy images of animals on the tar.
under the spell of childhood, me and the kids from next door
govern imagined worlds made of backyard scraps
until the sun goes down again

Things that no one notices
jolted rhythm of a cricket's jingle,
rustle of leaves as a grasshopper leaps into nothingness.
everything alive announces itself aloud
death only knows our silences

Thembe Mvula is a South African born writer and performance poet currently based in London. Her prize shortlisted debut poetry pamphlet, *We That Wither Beneath* was self published in 2019. Thembe is currently a Barbican Young Poet.

Enclosure

Karen McCarthy Woolf

O England, boasted land of liberty,
With strangers still thou mayst thy title own
But thy poor slaves the alteration see
With many a loss to them the truth is known
     'Enclosure', John Clare

O England, boasted land of liberty
Of palms drummed strong on pink & gristled chests
Of lawns landscaped to rust, liverish
as dogs' piss in summer's drought, windswept

& observed on closed & uptight circuits
— where one good eye's enough. How erotic!
Always to be watched, while we slept
through hurricanes & other chaotic

procedures. Our demise a triptych
on the walls of multi-storey, glassy cathedrals:
the centre panel a tissue of idyllic
hills & hens clucking a corporate pastoral,

epic as it was causal.
On every treetop a crow, crowned
a survivor, guzzling from oily puddles
while worthless Kings allowed

Nothing & Everything so kleptocracy flowered
bloody as exploded capillaries*
*exponential detonations designed to devour
all forms of flesh & resistance, bodily

or otherwise. O Walled World of disparity
& hard surfaces— Of barbed
fences augmented by engineered despair
& steel cages. Where algorithmic swords

pierce skin, gluttonous for the gruel of hard
knocks. Behold the petal, silky & violet!
Only bees ignore the buzz of armed
response: systems to keep each Eden inviolate.

Every lavender bush & cactus flower is private.
Do not pick the fruit! A pilfered blackberry
is a sin that stains this age of ordered disquiet.
In America, O, boasted land of liberty!

Karen McCarthy Woolf's poetry collections include *An Aviary of Small Birds* (2014) and *Seasonal Disturbances* (2017). She is also an editor, critic and radio dramatist. Usually based in London, she is currently a Fulbright All Disciplines post-doctoral Scholar at UCLA, as Writer in Residence at the Promise Institute for Human Rights Law.

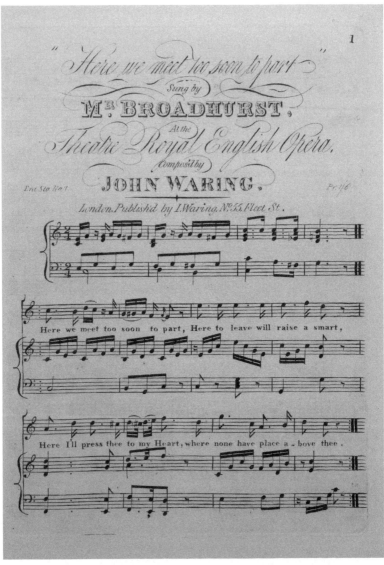

"Here we meet too soon to part" Sung by Mr. Broadhurst, At the Theatre Royal English Opera, Composed by John Waring (London: I. Waring, no date), p. 1.

Poems from Manchester Central Library
Edited by Clare Shaw

One day I turned up in your outdoor sink

Pam Schwarz

I came from no-where.
I was just in the air
or the clear water
you carried from the Furnace Pond.
I lived near your childhood place.
I can't swim or fly.
Instead, I have to live on a surface
or float.
I have a one-legged thing to move with
which I contract and relax in a ripple motion.
If you prod me I'll go back into my shell.
I'll line up with the others, resting too.

Waiting.

Pam Schwarz, born in Sussex, educated in Aberdeen, matured in Swaziland and tempered in Manchester. Founder member of Postcards from Pluto, a peer group of poets giving feedback and mutual support and encouraging study of published poets.

Caught in the Deep

Len Evans

I was silver and gold and large
in the bigger hands of Victor.

His halfway-house friend,
with a Banksy beard,
took a photo of us, then hurled
me back into the dirty canal.

Panicked, I accelerated away
and swallowed something green,
then something red.

I can't tire of swimming,
the alternative is worse.
So I've acclimatised to the rust
and the stink and the cold.

The towpath is full of photographers
shouting at me to smile.

Len Evans. Early enthusiasm for William Blake. Loves Italian and other opera. Shortlisted for Huddersfield Poetry Prize, 2010. Founder of Postcards for Pluto, peer group of poets giving feedback and mutual support and encouraging study of other poets.

Absence

Claire Burn

That first horse-kick to my stomach sent me   reeling
then winded me into the silence of
shock, of not feeling enough.
The silence of you

no longer breathing and the scent of you   gone.
Overtures and movements overtook me,
engulfed me in disbelief.
When the Sun's on my face it can be easy   until

wind and hail hunch my back
and force my head down
Sorry For Your Loss tossed
Congratulations straight off the mantle

as if I'd been careless, had I really misplaced   you?
Bureaucracy dictated that your birth certificate and
certificate of death
were written in the same hand

on the same day.
You remain under my skin and the dance goes on.
I've sat it out awhile   until

the next movement builds.
Exquisite refrains resound in my cells,
chords of resolution restore me   before
the plunging   discordant   tympanic   pounding

I   am   A l o n e

until quietly I gather myself up
turn down the volume
and pick up the steps, remembering how
to dance on   my own.

I have spent most of my life in Exmoor national park, the last two years in the Yorkshire Dales and I have a new appreciation of the landscape and nature because of this move. The opportunity provided by the John Clare workshops, to explore my poetry and myself.

Dearest John

Mary Matusz

Relish knowing countless birds are here,
their nest-building not so rare. In my garden
House Sparrows are common, Robins come
too and Coal Tits feast on seeds and crumbs.
Resident Blackbirds sing and every Spring
a pair of Collared Doves collects twigs, stalks.

I will tell you a strange thing;
towns and villages have swelled and some
people build wooden fences taller than me.
The poor red fox cannot fly over, hedgehogs
blocked from roaming the land to find supper.
I saw only one hedgehog these past two-years.
It all leaves a sour taste on my tongue.

I have heard there is a sanctuary
for orphaned hedgehogs in the next valley.
I have a mind to adopt a pair, build a little house
in the grass near the hedgerow, where thoughts
of Summer bring daisies, white clover, camomile
and a tingle to my neck.

Stories have multiplied since you were here
about the almost-have-beens, but let's be clear,
we're working on keeping them here, John Clare,
like the Skylark of your youth, the moths,
the butterflies you knew.

Walking with John Clare

Suzanne Batty

and you grew so much into the love of woods running
to dizzy yourself with head thrown back colours of leaf-birth
you stole into each glorious day in another creature's mind
its strangeness spreading through you like pure lichen
climbed the silver and blackwork of a birch to sit up high alone
so much song sun warming watery fields cuckoo's metronome
down in the valley the rhythm of all the greetings and leavings

you believed you could hear the secret language of trees
had yourself set the sun to catch on a chiffchaff's breast
to light up a mossy treecreeper – everything seemed to be rushing
from the broken to the mended so you went on with your constant fall
and recover moving bodily through the world aware of your lengthening
shadow your hands raised not in a gesture of surrender but
to swat away death to stop it landing

oh but when they took you away you found all the woods vanished
hedges hacked down monotony of brickwork agitation of sky
a blackbird building its desperate nest in the dank asylum courtyard –
5 pairs of blinking eyes amongst the tattered roses until those servant-styled
keepers came with shears and saws to clear the tangling
they made you stop all your sleeping rough eating grass lying down
by the stream like a poet promised to make everything quieten
even the sprawling memory of boys throwing earth over the stopped
body of a hawk they had killed the lies they told you

you were imprisoned kindly offered seclusion and restraint they only
   shook you
when you cried over starlings sparrows yellowhammers disappearing
   into smog
What's the use they said of begging birds to sing of resurrection?
We know the last skulk of foxes are afraid but even you John Clare
can't tell us how to reach the horizon to look down into a new world

Suzanne Batty's most recent poetry collection *States of Happiness* (Bloodaxe 2018)
was one of The Guardian's poetry books of the year. She won the Poetry Society's
Anne Born prize in its inaugural year. She uses creative writing to work with people
experiencing and recovering from mental distress.

Heading Home

Alan Spencer

I come from a pot-holed crescent
where a faulty street lamp
strobed the fur
of moon-savvy cats;

a post box sunk
in a tarred-brick wall,
its red mouth hard
as a Russian winter.

I come from a house
with a peeling milk-crate
on a cracked doorstep,
cobwebbed with memories
and dried-up flies.

I come from a kitchen
with fake-marble tops,
a whitewashed larder
stocked with greens.

I come from ribs and cabbage,
Goblin meat puddings,
Bird's trifles and Vesta Chow Mein.

Saturday nights at Ferranti's club -
the Gay Gordons, the Virginia Reel,
a hiss of cymbals
as the glitter ball whirled.

On the way home with an oily curry,
cats scrapped in a pitch-dark alley,
teeth sank through flesh
into bone.

Alan Spencer's poems appeared in several poetry magazines, including *Rain Dog*, *Brittle Star*, *Orbis* and *Sarasvati*, and two anthologies: *Transparency* (Crocus 2005) and *The Best of Manchester Poets Vol. 1* (Puppywolf 2010). His first collection *The Lodger* was published by Indigo Dreams in 2009. Tragically, Alan died in the spring of 2020, just as we started preparing this book for publication.

To Create Anew

Mary Gavin

I love to write –

the pen in my hand,
the paper connecting with ink,

the wood from the tree
still shedding its leaves

of love
so long after
it was cut down,

living again in a
new form

and unconditionally
still loving

that which
cut it.

Mary has loved writing from being a child. She has a passion for language and its
ability to connect and heal. Now retired from teaching she writes poetry and short
stories and edits work from University students. Her poetry has found a natural
home in many multicultural and interfaith events.

A Prayer for the Carers

J Ahmed

A prayer for the carers
who truly give their all;
to help the people, who in need
upon them, they do call.

Their kindly, loving hearts
to help and to protect
in a world which suffers deeply
where people do neglect.

A prayer for the carers
who keep the world working,
whilst people turn their eye away
from those that are deserving;
The carer never turns away
or bats an eye at all.
The carer is the one
who helps everyone stand tall.

A prayer for the carer
who has no airs and graces;
who stops to keep a watchful eye
on people in their spaces.
Lovingly, their time they share,
in doing so they give;
caring is the meaning
and the reason that they live...

A poet from Salford, I have always had a keen interest in the work of John Clare.
Recently, I have reignited my relationship with his poetry – this has inspired many
new pieces.

I love

Christina Wilson

I love
to wake at night and walk at dawn. I tread through the sleeping town in a gust of seaweed. By the harbour, the fishermen stack lobster creels: I stand wordless with icy wrists. The sky contracts in pink swells; two fisherman sail east in their night-lit boat. A lighthouse flashes its heartbeat. A seagull whimpers, suspended above me as light spreads.

The sky expands as it births the sun. In a slit of scarlet the horizon stretches open. Light emerges as day, celebrated in yellows. I walk home through the bay's graveyard of benches, each inscribed with its own memorial. They sit overlooking the spot where children pop seaweed pouches, next to the old outdoor swimming pool.

I pass the doocot, empty pigeon-fortress now housing damp. Glowing cracks press out of curtain-drawn windows, veiling a mother who fed her baby by night, crying for the darkness to end. Both sleep as the sky shines silver and grey. I hear the rattle of a delivery van in the sprawl of the waves forming and reforming. I turn a key in my front door, cord clamped and cut. *In the beginning I was there.*

Christina lives in West Yorkshire. She enjoys the feeling of pen moving on paper and the warmth of books. Christina has an MA in Creative Writing and celebrates the therapeutic benefits of writing, working to share the benefits of writing and creativity in her facilitation of therapeutic writing workshops.

Salmon

Kate Bevan

I rush with the flow …
                 downwards
then, up… *up… UP*

through the grasses,
through the current,
through the night-stars' guidance
through the pull of the moon-magnet
the swell and estuary, streams
salt-less and more

till I re-find my flow in the river
up and up onwards
life depends on it
through the detritus of beer tops
and nylon-net rubbish
through ditches still damp
I reclaim my last act
to spawn against Nature's lost cause.

Kate Bevan lives in Bolton. Her storytelling seeks 'voice' for the 'othered'. Her background in art, environment; politics, communications and radio inform collaborative works: CFCCA Manchester; Gabriel Fine Arts, London. Contributor: STEPZ II; Fruitful Futures, Platforma Festival, Beat the Border, Words of Hope NHS. She delivers workshops for the LOGIK Centre, Leeds.

Carers

Angi Holden

Gratitude for the holders of hands, whose firm grip
stills the shaking. Gratitude for the bedside hours,
the pouring of cool water, the holding
of beakers, the spooners of mush.
Gratitude for the listeners, for those who
bend their heads, who catch the faint words
of the sick and dying. Gratitude for the imaginative,
the ones who talk about how it was back then,
even though they'd not been born.

Gratitude for the night workers,
who allow the sons and daughters respite,
who hold their places for an hour or two.

And afterwards, gratitude for the ones
who bend the rules, who share a hug,
a cup of tea, a plain sweet biscuit.
Gratitude to those who say her passing
was peaceful, who gloss over the dry lips
and the rattling breath, the ones who say
her time had come, that she was ready.

Angi Holden's poetry and fiction, widely published online and in print, explores the environment, family history and personal experience. Her pamphlet *Spools of Thread* (2018) won the inaugural Mother's Milk Pamphlet Prize. Her short story *Painting Stones for Virginia* (2018) was a prize winner in the Cheshire Prize for Literature.

Wakening

John Mills

Just as shell gives way
to the beak's insistence
new growth cracks the ground
as winter withdraws

Blossom and manure mark the air
that grows comfy with warmth.
Hedges, edged with music,
thicken with leaf and nest.

Frost aches for dew.
Bough burns for bud
Cob pines for pen
Fox sniffs for vixen

The air, the earth, the water,
sing with a loose, bubbly, trill;
softer than a Cirl Bunting
quicker than a Whitethroat.

Note: the final lines are quoted from Peter Hayman and Rob Hume, *The Complete Guide to the Birdlife of Britain and Europe* (2001).

Former teacher John is a published prize winner, and he is never afraid to explore 'The Dark Places'. Helen Mort describes his work as, 'compassionate, bold and generous', and Jean Atkin his reading, 'barnstorming'. He recently gained an MA with Distinction from Keele University.

The Fish Quines

Liz Mills

They knew us by our smell.

All the way from Stornaway we'd go each Spring,
following the Silver Darlings to Shetland
then down as far as Lowestoft
before the long journey home for the winter.

The three of us worked and slept together
- me and Chrissie and our cousin Morag.
She was tall, so she packed while we gutted,
singing and laughing as we bent over the farlins.

The days were long and the work was hard,
but oh! the company was fine.
Always other lassies to share a joke with
and the deck hands to eye up.

We'd race each other to fill the barrels;
we could fillet seven hundred in ten minutes
and our cutags would shine like the herring
or the shilling we'd see for each one we filled.

We followed the fish...
and talk to the crews
them dreaming of boats and us of houses.
We were good girls, though our tongues were sharp

and our hands were aye so sore!
We'd try to ease the cuts that even our clouties couldn't cover.
On the Sabbath we'd listen to the Minister
as we hid their redness and our thoughts from the boys.

Liz Mills has been on stage interpreting other people's words for sixty years or so, but has given up acting and teaching, and now enjoys performing her own work. She was born in Yorkshire, brought up in the far North of Scotland and now lives in Staffordshire.

Through Norsey Fields

Nigel King

Two cows in the distance, moving slowly.
The sun high overhead.

A cowpat, dried to a rough disk of crust,
warm and sludgy underneath.

A bluebottle, thrilled at the scent
– a maniac's buzzing chainsaw.

Down by the stream, the woodpigeon's call.
A scrabbling deep in the brambles.

Crow feathers caught on barbed wire
The reek of fox by the stile.

Ashes from last night's fire.
Empty cans of Skol and Harp.

Gliding through the long grass,
the black zigzag backs of snakes.

Nigel King lives in Almondbury, Huddersfield, though grew up in Essex – school
trips to Epping Forest are his closest connection to John Clare! He is the author
of *What I Love About Daleks* (Calder Valley Poetry) and has been published in
magazines such as *Poetry Salzburg Review, Pennine Platform* and *Algebra of Owls*.

Some Men (for John Clare)

Clare Shaw

Some men go out very late at night
to look for it. They see it in trees
with the moonlight on it; they shout to it.
Some walk many miles to be with it.
Though they cannot reach it,
they remember it all their lives; it drives them

mad. Some find it in fields
and their word is mud, some wish to be free
of it. Other men carry the key to it and never know.
Some men know only the ghost of it.
They hear it in woods and they run from it.
Some men are born to it, some men are taught it,

others must teach themselves.
Some men would fight for the prize of it,
others are jumped by it, wounded and floored by it.
But some men can walk right through it
as though they are in a dream, they fear no evil.
Some men have seen the whole world

fall and reform around them
and cannot find their place in it. A few know the language
of birds: they may pay a high price for it.
Some are fairly contented without it
but some wake every day and they ache for it,
weep for the lack of it. They are birds

and they cannot fly. Some men will not know
their children or wives when they see them,
but some men see things as they are:
birds sing there, they hear them.
Some men know they are kings.
But no-one believes them.

Clare Shaw: I'm a Bloodaxe poet, with three collections and a fourth on the way. Often addressing political and personal conflict, my poetry is fuelled by my faith in the transformative and redemptive power of language. I'm a passionate mental health activist, and I've written and spoken extensively about the role of language in mental health provision. Other projects include a national collaboration with the Royal Literary Fund and USDAW, the retail and distribution union, to bring creativity and writing skills into workplaces. John Clare's work captures – with joy, brilliance and heartbreak – my own fascination with identity, class, the working life, psychological suffering and the natural world.

HERE WE MEET TOO SOON TO PART.

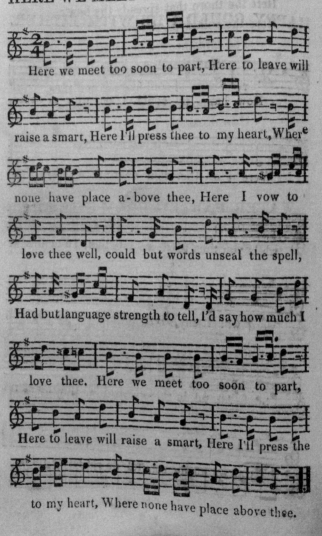

Here we meet too soon to part, Here to leave will

raise a smart, Here I'll press thee to my heart, Where

none have place a-bove thee, Here I vow to

love thee well, could but words unseal the spell,

Had but language strength to tell, I'd say how much I

love thee. Here we meet too soon to part,

Here to leave will raise a smart, Here I'll press the

to my heart, Where none have place above thee.

'Here we meet too soon to part', in [Anon.], *The Sky-Lark: A Choice Selection of the Most Admired Popular Songs, Heroic, Plaintive, Sentimental, Humourous, and Baccanalian. Arranged for the Violin, Flute and Voice.* (London: Thomas Tegg, 1825), p. 112.

Clare, as poet *and* musician: some anniversary thoughts

Julian Philips

So it's two hundred years since the publication of Clare's *Poems Descriptive of Rural Life & Scenery* in 1820, a year that turned out to be the high point of Clare's worldly fame. It's also two hundred years since the first musical setting of a Clare poem, 'The Meeting', by Haydn Corri (1785–1860), and performed by the acclaimed mezzo soprano, Madame Vestris at Covent Garden. Clare, on his first visit to London, famously missed it – 'we was to have but it was too late'.

A shame he did, as I would love to know what Clare made of Cori's setting. After all, Clare was a fluent and accomplished musician, his fiddle-playing rewarded with a Cremona violin from publisher James Hessey. In full lyric poet mode, Clare was often writing words for music, but here was Corri writing music for Clare's words. What would he have made of the song? Corri's tune could hardly be said to fully encapsulate the layers of Clare's poem, and it's hard to see how verses two and three quite fit. Maybe the music is just a little too genteel, word and note too politely separated like figures across a drawing room, when for Clare, music and text were so closely entwined. Clare's early life must have been full of the ballads, dances and folk songs from a rich oral tradition where little was noted down, most material passed on and reshaped through performance. As George Deacon puts it, these folk songs were 'neither poems with music nor tunes with incidental words; they should be seen as complete in themselves'.[1] So for Clare, perhaps, there was always music in his words.

Many a composer since Corri in 1820 has sought to put Clare's words into music, though in his lifetime Clare's lyric poetry failed to inspire a flowering of English song analogous to the *Lieder* of Clare's great contemporary, Franz Schubert. In his *John Clare Society Journal* article of 1982, Trevor Hold lists just *Winter's Gone* by William Sterndale Bennett (1856) but then later works by established twentieth-century British composers such as Peter Warlock, Benjamin Britten, or Malcolm Arnold; more contemporary settings include works by Tansy Davies, Anthony Gilbert or Brian Elias. My own fascination with Clare began with a choral setting of *Song's Eternity* in 2002, and continued with two song cycles for voice and piano: *Four Sonnets of John Clare* (2015) and *Love Songs for Mary Joyce* (2016). Somehow the inner music of Clare's poetry releases a kind of creative oxygen, and for all the complexities Clare's poetry presents – its rhythmic intricacies, its breathless unpunctuated lines – he is a poet I keep returning to, striving to ensure that music and text are as closely entwined as they must have been in Clare's creative imagination.

Perhaps inevitably considering the powerful contemporary resonances of Clare's legacy, this Clare fascination has been pushing at the boundaries of circumscribed musical forms such as song or choral settings. For some years I've wanted to develop larger-scale work around Clare, drawing together spoken/sung text, instrumental music, video and field recordings. So with Simon Kövesi, actor Toby Jones, producer Kate Romano, writer Stephen Plaice and director Caroline Clegg, we've been developing ideas – not opera, not conventional narrative, but creative approaches which keep music and text close together, allowing us to explore Clare's themes with wider audiences: the natural world, the human heart, mind and body, landscape and place, mortality.

And yet how do we find frameworks for exploring Clare's many preoccupations? Clare's output is rich and vast, his poetry extraordinarily varied, his verse forms diverse, sometimes self-contained enough to allow a composer to make a conventional song-setting, sometimes dizzyingly open-ended. Increasingly I see Clare as a radical, almost experimental figure, where the flow of his poetry's inner music is more important than the structures that contain it. So instead of focussing on form, I've been focussing on just making musical material, trusting that our collaborative process will enable the material to find its shape. I've been working on a set of art-songs, a variation sequence based on Corri's *The Meeting* that culminates in my own setting of the same poem, and a set of creative folk song transcriptions, some instrumental, some vocal, based on the tunes and lyrics that Clare collected himself.

In the 1820s, during the period of his early fame, Clare 'pricked down' over 260 of the 'hundreds of … pleasant tunes familiar to the plough & the splashing st[r]eam & the little fields of spring'. Beautifully written out, these books of fiddle tunes give us a wonderful insight into Clare the musician – is the violin introduction to 'Black Ey'd Susan' an example of

Clare the composer? And are the notational irregularities 'mistakes' on Clare's part, or a genuine attempt to capture the spontaneity of the live performance of an oral, non-notated, tradition?

I've chosen nine of Clare's fiddle tunes, which could be woven into the fabric of a show, including this beautiful tune:

Young Huzzar

A 'pleasant tune' indeed: simple and diatonic, with an easy flow, and disarmingly ear-catching. It's as if Clare collected it just as he closely observed a primrose, violet or cowslip and I've tried to inform my creative transcriptions in a similar spirit, letting the tune speak/sing within the context of my own creative imagination. With 'Young Huzzar', I divided the melody into two layers – one for clarinet, one for violin – with the layers first alternating separately:

for Livvy and Kate

Young Huzzar

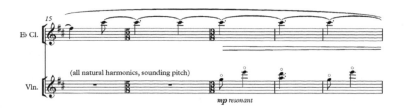

before coming together to form the complete tune, the timbre of the small Eb clarinet and high violin harmonics creating a music box effect:

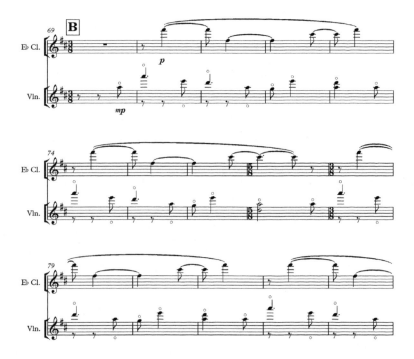

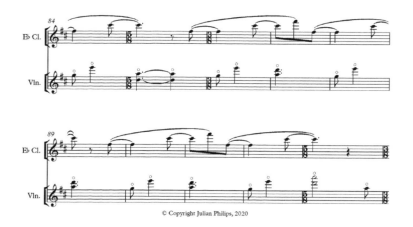

In this way, I've worked on eight other Clare tunes, and the experience has given me a very different perspective on his poetry. Looking at his musical notation has allowed me a glimpse into the mind of Clare the musician, which in turn has created a collaborative space within which I can work. So many of his idiosyncrasies as a poet might well relate back to his engagement with the music of folk songs and dances where material is never fixed, but constantly in flux, reshaped from one performance context to another. I hope very much that whatever the show we might be able to make, we will be able to explore Clare in this way, as poet *and* musician, as a strong contribution to the richly renewing debate around this extraordinary figure.

The work of composer Julian Philips ranges widely across stage and concert hall, his output evidencing a long-established concern for the interrelationship between music and text, whether in song, dance or opera. Philips was Glyndebourne Festival Opera's first composer-in-residence (2006-10), which culminated in his acclaimed youth opera *Knight Crew* (2010), and chamber opera *The Yellow Sofa* (2009); *The Tale of Januarie* (2017), based on Chaucer's *Merchant's Tale*, was the first opera created in middle English. John Clare has long been a source of fascination for Philips resulting in his anthem *Song's Eternity* (2002), and song cycles *Four Sonnets of John Clare* (2015) and *Love Songs for Mary Joyce* (2016). Julian is Head of Composition at the Guildhall School of Music and Drama.

NOTES

1   George Deacon, *John Clare and the Folk Tradition* (London: Francis Boutle, 2002. First pub. 1983).

THE SKYLARK.

Above the russet clods, the corn is seen
Sprouting its spiry points of tender green,
Where squats the hare, to terrors wide awake,
Like some brown clod the harrows failed to break.
Opening their golden caskets to the sun,
The buttercups make schoolboys eager run,
To see who shall be first to pluck the prize—
Up from their hurry see the Skylark flies,
And o'er her half-formed nest, with happy wings
Winnows the air, till in the cloud she sings,
Then hangs a dust spot in the sunny skies,
And drops, and drops, till in her nest she lies,
Which they unheeded passed—not dreaming then
That birds, which flew so high, would drop again
To nests upon the ground, which any thing
May come at to destroy.   Had they the wing
Like such a bird, themselves would be too proud,
And build on nothing but a passing cloud!
As free from danger, as the heavens are free
From pain and toil, there would they build, and be,
And sail about the world to scenes unheard
Of and unseen,—O were they but a bird!
So think they, while they listen to its song,
And smile, and fancy, and so pass along;
While its low nest, moist with the dews of morn,
Lies safely, with the leveret, in the corn.

Facsimile of 'The Skylark', from *The Rural Muse, Poems by John Clare*
(London: Whittaker & Co., 1835), p. 83.

The Fallen Elm: extract

Stephen Plaice

The following monologue is section of a larger dramatic work *The Fallen Elm*, an audience with John Clare in the Northampton General Lunatic Asylum. The year is 1854 and visitors have come to visit 'the peasant poet' in his madness as their Sunday entertainment. In this section, Clare speaks to them about his relationships with women, and refers to his 'two wives', Martha Turner Clare, known to him as 'Patty of the Vale', to whom he was indeed still legally married, and Mary Joyce, his 'spiritual wife' whom he had known since childhood. Patty never visited him in the asylum during his more than twenty-two year incarceration. Mary Joyce had already died as far back as 1838. Yet she continued to exist in Clare's imagination for many years, as if she were still alive.

The monologues are intended to be performed to a score by Julian Philips, which includes a number of direct settings of the poems.

Where I am quoting directly from Clare's poems and autobiographical writings I have kept his spelling and punctuation.

Johnny Two Wives

When I came to London
that first time
in the days of my fame,
there was so much,
the buildings, the bustle,
the horses thrashing the cobblestones,
I was uncommonly astonished
to see so many ladys
as I thought them
walking about the streets
I expressed my surprise
and was told they were girls of the town
as a modest woman rarely ventured
out by herself at nightfall.
It was like running behind the mail coach.
I couldn't catch up with it all.
On the street I would walk behind them,
hoping that when they turned round
I would not be attracted to them,
and feel the pain of not having them.
Instead, I wrote them all down.

I'd like to think it was London
that made me a ladys man,
but more likely it was in my nature,
like the ram.

As I grew up a man
I mixed more in company
and frequented dancings
for the sake of meeting with lasses
for I was a lover very early in life.

he pictures his youth

'Some pretty face
remembered in our youth
seems ever with us
whispering love and truth.'

I must write that down.
he does, writing so furiously the pencil breaks
The impressions come so fast
I press so hard the point breaks on my pencil.
Sometimes you can put the lead back in again,
sometimes you can't.
he tries and fails to repair his pencil

My first attachment was a schoolboy affection
Mary – who cost me more ballads than sighs –
was belovd with a romantic or platonic sort of feeling
 if I could but gaze on her face
or fancy a smile on her countenance
it was sufficient
I went away satisfied
we playd with each other
but nothing named of love
yet I fancyd her eyes told me her affections
we walked together as school companions
yet young as my heart was
it woud turn chill
when I touched her hand
and trembled and I fancyd
her feelings were the same
for as I gazed earnestly in her face
a tear woud hang in her smiling eye
and she woud turn to whipe it away
her heart was tender as a birds
but when she grew up to woman hood
she felt her station above mine
at least I felt that she thought so
for her parents were farmers
and farmers had great pretensions to something then
so my passion coold with my reason
and contented itself with another
tho I felt a hopful tenderness
one that I might one day renew the acquaintance
and disclose the smotherd passion
she was a beautiful girl, my Mary,
and as the dream awoke into reality
her beauty was always fresh in my memory...
she is still unmarried...

There were lots of lasses after Mary
I'd see a pretty girl
scribble a song in her praise
spend a couple of innocent
and harmless Sundays with her
then move on to the next,
but then there was Betty,
with her glossy black curls
and hazel eyes.
It began with a heedless fumbling
at Stamford Fair.

They ask me who I love the best
But who I never tell
and when I laugh among the rest
I think of Betty Sell

They ask me who my heart preferred
& much on duty dwell
I never say a single word
but think of Betty Sell

They talk of who their hearts has won
But mine I never tell
and look as if I knew of none
But think of Betty Sell

pause

We always remember our first, don't we,
I can see you thinking of them now –
I'll give you a moment.

he does

But by then I had already met Martha
'Patty of the Vale' I used to call her
the woman who would become my wife
I remember the tree under which we met
the shady spot she first smiled at me
on the way into Stamford
I spoke with her and was so bold
as to help her over the stile

and walk her to her cottage four miles off.
This became the introduction
to some of the happiest and unhappiest days
my life has met with.

Between you, me and the gatepost,
I think it was because of Betty
she let me in, over her stile, so to speak,
and then in two shakes of a lamb's tail
she was with child.
Then I knew I had to let go of Betty
and her dark curls,
but I never let go of her
in my mind. Not quite.
She keeps going round in my head,
like the fish that got away.
You always remember that
more clearly than the one you actually caught,
don't you madam?
You're thinking about him now.
I can tell.

Oh, I loved Patty well enough.
She worked hard
and kept a clean house.
But it didn't stop me wanting other lasses.
Quite the contrary.

he is lost in memory for a moment

Even on the way back from London
the very day I was minded
to ask Patty to marry me,
because she was heavy with my child,
I teased up the pretty serving girl
who pulls the beer in the Bull at Ware
I bussed her on the cheek.
Have you seen her?

he is picturing her in his mind

Such beauties she has.
Like hills of snow.

he returns to the audience

Ah, we put up the banns,
Patty and me,
and before I knew it I was back
hedging for a living,
just some ordinary hodge
fit only to be a ditcher
and a limeburner again.
Trouble is my own people
had turned against me.
They thought I'd given myself London airs
and was too good for them.
Except the girls that is –
the ones who had never given me a second look before,
now gave me plenty, thinking maybe
I was their ticket out of the fens.

Temptations were things
I rarely resisted
when the partiality of the moment
or the strength of the beer
gave no time for reflection
I was sure to seize it
whatever might be the consequence

I was led by profligate companions
and coaxed about to bad houses
where not only my health but my life
has been on the eve of its sacrifice
by an illness too well-known
and too disgusting to mention.

It might be that has put me in here,
the doctor won't say.
I have these fits and these sores sometimes.
I see the Blue Devils.
It's a punishment from God.
For being mucky around those saucies.
But marriage was a punishment too.

Like I had my Don Juan say:
'Marriage is nothing but a driveling hoax
To please old codgers when they're turned of forty
I wed and left my wife like other folks
But not until I found her false and faulty
O woman fair – the man must pay thy jokes
Such makes a husband very often naughty
Who falls in love will seek his own undoing
The road to marriage is "the road to ruin"'.

It didn't suit me.
At night I fancied she stole my body heat
and left me weak in the morning.
Six children Martha gave me.
I loved 'em all.
But I couldn't keep the hearth.
I strayed.

I have two wives now,
doesn't everybody really,
in their heads at least?
Be honest sir, don't you.
You might live with one in your house,
but you live with another
in your imagination, don't you.
I can see it in your face.
Johnny Two Wives you can call me.
Mine are Martha and Mary.
Martha, my domestic wife,
the one I call Patty,
and Mary, my spirit-wife.
Patty never visits here.
It's too far to come now she says,
and she has to look after the children.
As if peering in through the window
Ah yes. They are all still there in the cottage.

Pause.

Mary doesn't come to visit me either.

madder

They took from me my wife and to save trouble
I wed again and made the error double

madder still

'I have two wives and I should like to see them
Both by my side before another hour
If both are honest I should like to be them
For both are fair and bonny as a flower
And one o Lord – *(aside)* now do bring in the tea mem –
were bards pens steamers each of ten horse power
I could not bring her beautys fair to weather
So I've towed both in harbour blest together'

pause

Nah. I haven't touched a woman in ten years.
Instead I've had to remember
all the ones I knew back then.
I made a list.
Have you ever made a list
of all the ones you've honeyed?
I'll give you a moment.

pause while the audience counts

Let the dog see the rabbit.
I can see that lady over there
has already run out of fingers
to count on,
and if we wait for you sir
we'll be here all night, won't we.
So I will continue.

I'm fifth class in here,
so I can go abroad.
I amble into town most days,
sit in the portico of All Saints
that's my favourite spot.
I make lists of girls there too,
the ones the local lads tell me about.
I'll write them a poem

for a screw of baccy to chew,
so they can pass the verses off
as their own to their lasses.
I have to write down their names
in case I forget who I am wooing.

Before I was here
I was in Dr Allen's private asylum in Essex.
Hard to believe but
Lord Tennyson had one of the front rooms.
My tongue was too tied to speak to him.
He was a real poet, after all,
Queen Victoria said so,
not a rhyming clown like me.
She's made him the Laureate now.

When I was in Dr Allen's asylum
there I had a mind to escape
because I wanted to see my wives,
Mary above all, but when I got home
they told me she was dead
these eight years past.
I said that couldn't be true
as I've been speaking to her all this time
I saw her going about Langley Bush
just yesterday, didn't I?

So I wrote to her to let her know
I had returned home from Essex

'To Mary Clare – Glinton Northborough the 27th of July 1841

My dear wife

I have written an account of my journey
or rather escape from Essex for your amusement
and hope it may divert your leisure hours –
I would have told you before now that I got here
to Northborough last friday night
but not being able to see you
or to hear where you was
I soon began to feel homeless at home

and shall bye and bye feel near hopeless
but not so lonely as I did in Essex –
for here I can see Glinton Church
and feeling that Mary is safe if not happy
and I am gratified though my home is no home to me
my hopes are not entirely hopeless
while even the memory of Mary lives so near me
God Bless you my dearest Mary
Your affectionate husband

John Clare'

Patty always said
chasing after all these women
I was just searching for my twin.
Ah. Bessey. My twin.
She had barely lived a month out of the womb.

'Bessey – I call thee by that earthly name
That but a little while belonged to thee –
Thou left me growing up to sin and shame
And kept thy innocence untained and free
To meet the refuge of a heaven above
Where life's bud opens in eternity'

pause

But I never found her.
My twin sister.

I can see that gentleman over there
is still counting his conquests.
He hasn't heard a word I've said.

***

Stephen Plaice is a poet and dramatist. An internationally-renowned librettist, he has written verse librettos for Sir Harrison Birtwistle. Michael Zev Gordon, Luis Tinoco, Julian Grant, Julian Philips, Orlando Gough and many other notable contemporary composers. From 1987 to 1994, he was Writer-in-Residence at Lewes Prison in Sussex. Stephen is currently Writer-in-Residence and Professor of Dramatic Writing at the Guildhall School of Music and Drama in London. His selected poems *Those Under Saturn* were published by Parvenu Press in 2018. His sequence of novels *The Hardham Divine* will be published in 2021.

Acknowledgements

Simon Kövesi

I would like to thank colleagues at Oxford Brookes University, for support and backing for this project, especially Katharine Craik, Christina Beck, Mike Henderson, Kim Shadbolt, Dina Sikorska, Joseph Carr, Joanna Cooksey, Gary Browning, Laura Baldock, Dave McPhee, Brian Rivers, Thomas Shepherd, Kirsty McNally, Paul Whitty, Niall Munro, Dan Lea, Irène Hill, Simon White, Eric White and Rachael Langford. Thanks to Jonathan Douglas and Fay Lant at the National Literacy Trust for early advice and encouragement. My thanks to the keen energies and promotional abilities of all librarians and administrators at Bradford Libraries, Peterborough Central Library (Vivacity) and Peterborough Museum, Manchester Central Library, and all at Lambeth Libraries – Clapham Library, in particular: Dionne Hood, Elaine Wilkinson, Stacey Kennedy, Richard Hunt, Glenys Wass, Danny Middleton, Tim O'Dell and Arthur Lech respectively.

Thanks to Toby Jones for being so committed to the project from our very first conversation about it. Thanks to all on the John Clare Society committee – most especially to the Chair, the magnificent Dr Valerie Pedlar. Thanks to David Knotts for crucial early advice, to Poppy Corbett for ongoing dramaturgical wisdom, and to Don Sloan of the Oxford Cultural Collective also for early advice. I am lucky to know many kind, brilliant scholars of Clare – and for this project I repeatedly drew on the generosity and wisdom of Erin Lafford, Fiona Stafford, Kirsteen McCue, Sam Ward, Scott McEathron, Kelsey Thornton, Bridget Keegan and John Goodridge, among many others. And thanks to my collaborators in the project itself – the final fruition of which is still to come: centrally, poets Sarah Corbett, John Gallas, Karen McCarthy Woolf, and Clare Shaw; actor Toby Jones; producer Kate Romano; composer Julian Philips; playwright Stephen Plaice; and director Caroline Clegg. For the cover – commissioned and designed during lockdown as so much of this book was – my thanks to Glasgow artist and critic, Mitch Miller, the Dialectograms maestro.

The kernel of this project was formed as a kind of answer to questions in my book – about how Clare works creatively in the here and now – about what such work means about history, and about his specific story; and it is also a response to the work I have enjoyed doing with and alongside creative artists of all kinds – specifically in editing the *John Clare Society Journal* since 2008, in running the 'John Clare in Space' conference at Oxford Brookes in May 2014, and most significantly in taking part in the *By Our Selves* project (feature film, book, exhibition, merry dances), across 2014 and 2015. To Andrew and Eden Kötting, Iain Sinclair, the late, great Freddie Jones, MacGillivray, Jem Finer, David Aylward, Alan Moore – indeed to all contemporary artists and writers who have worked so attentively on Clare (Brian Shields, David Morley, Carry Akroyd among many others) I owe a deep debt of thanks, for all the loosening inspiration, without which this project could not have happened.

Our deepest sympathies go to the friends and family of our Manchester Central Library workshop poet, Alan Spencer, who appears in Clare Shaw's section on p. 55. Sadly, Alan died in the spring of 2020, so never saw this book published.